Hollow Shell

Holly Mastyla

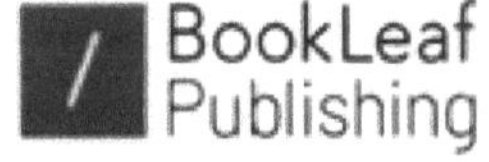

Hollow Shell © 2023 Holly Mastyla

All rights reserved.

No part of this publication may be reproduced, stored in a retrieval system, or transmitted, in any form or by any means, electronic, mechanical, photocopying, recording or otherwise, without the prior written permission of the presenters.

Holly Mastyla asserts the moral right to be identified as author of this work.

Presentation by *BookLeaf Publishing*

Web: www.bookleafpub.com

E-mail: info@bookleafpub.com

ISBN: 9789357213103

First edition 2023

Bright Memories

Sit back and relax, sip your glass of wine
Think back to childhood, running around blind
Innocent and free, always on cloud nine
Draw back the drapes and dream with the
sunshine

Wasted Potential

2

Words and phrases that seem so prophetical
Blowing your mind with strings alphabetical
Maybe it's more of a theoretical
Cause in the end, it's just hypothetical

Mystery

3

Madness engulfing every thought
Young and old alike entranced
Struggling to solve the puzzles
Trying not to lose their minds
Everyone wants what they can't have
Rising up in droves, united
Yet few are truly masters of Mystery

Yeah, Science!

Creating prose or writing lyrics
No subject is without its critics
Sane studies or debunking mystics
Everything is a part of physics

Zeus' Papoose

5

Release the noose ya silly goose
They called a truce, don't be obtuse
Locked in deuce, may as well sluice
The time is abuse, that I did deduce
Not an excuse, they merely abduce
God please produce a giant papoose
To let us run loose, but fuck it's no use
Forever a recluse, kicked in the caboose
Shame, 'twas profuse, did not make the boy
spruce
Outside, a moose with which he did conduce
This life will not seduce, 'tis time for him to
vamoose

Dream of a Brighter Tomorrow

A conflict so great, left with contusions
The world spins and warps in your confusion
Winning the war was only delusion
Now peace only exists in illusions

The Myth of Serenity

When shadow meets the light, the demons break
free
When time begins anew, no one hears the plea
When Luna reigns, sanity is lost to thee
An eternal cycle will always haunt me

The Last Laugh

A sickening smile is all that is left. The
anarchy's gone, yet he feels bereft.
Every decision brought unending pain, yet he
brushed it off and acted insane.
The jokes were the enders of countless lives, but
it's still bittersweet to say goodbye.

Hollow Bonds

9

Endeavouring love persists evermore
Lonely heart fights in a forever war
Painful reflection by the river shore
A light in the dark with me nevermore

Human Nature

Heavy is the head that wears the crown
Cursed is the mind smart enough to frown
Pained is the soul without a breakdown
Always you'll find those fated to drown

Deep Breath

Remember the cries of joyous laughter
Living peacefully in blissful ignorance
Thinking all will live happily ever after

Then calamity struck with wrathful indifference
Red sky shadows the once calming green
The kingdom is purged of all innocence

Nation razed; civilians are few and far between
Monsters reign in this terminal hour
Rallying hope drowned out by the screams

Beasts fall to this divine power
Last vestiges of courage fade away
Wisdom perseveres and preserves a silent flower

Breathe in, focus, no time to delay
Breathe out, stand strong, and face the final day

Conflicted Conscience

Melodious world and joyous perfection
Bringing me such high hopes
Ruinous fate and insistent infection
Smother my neck with rope

Natural biology shows it's beauty
When something intakes air
Men wreak havoc on life and call it duty
Earth's in the crosshairs

Death and disease are a commonplace affair
And nobody bats an eye
The likeliest future is barren and bare
Can't even see the sky

There are chances for change, science can save
us
Look at all that we've done!
Protecting Gaia is our sworn mission, plus
We're not alone, we're one

Prime Directive

13

Size and strength can decide it all
But words are enough to make a grown man
small
Rougher times I'm unable to recall
One shall stand and one shall fall

The Rainbow Collection

Raging blood mixed with deceit
Healing vigor and courageous thrills
A lovely view of an evil treat
Blades of the rose cut sweetly still

Covetous envy or a tangy zest
A burning passion flares within
Signature sight in the wild west
Fruits of labour brings fire and sin

Ease and warmth of a summer's day
Joy expressed in musical visions
Neutral effects are easy to convey
Yet the fear brings about new conditions

The will of the wild casts a wide net
More chance for beauty to be seen
Danger lurks and all is a threat
It's not easy being green

Despair and darkness of sea and sky
A tear of sorrow cuts the rope
Calming waters can dry your eye
Contrastingly beautiful, ignite your hope

Judgemental blue plum ponders emotion
Ignoring you turns hearts ashen
The wise man sharply bears devotion
For it takes true strength to hold compassion

The cold allure of lilac peace
Brings about your ultimate fall
Poisonous power makes pride decrease
Give in to the light, for love conquers all

The Devil's Folly

16

Passing time as a wily trickster
Crushing souls like a raging twister
But a lonely thumb stopped this drifter
Leading to the birth of my sister

A Shadow's Cry

A weary mind watches you near
Broken soul with a guiding light
Burning pain; they cower in fear
Alone on a cold winter's night

Embers of hope flickering out
Spirit of the past still haunts them
Drowning sorrows to a blackout
Sunflower reduced to a stem

Engulfing beam takes you off course
Mirrored hearts meet and synchronise
Drawing out their pain from the source
Much deeper than you realise

Strangers once, but now family
You see through all of their shadows
Curtain closed with the finale
Bring rise to a blooming meadow

The darkness screeches in your face
The darkness fears your warm embrace

Happy Birthday

Another year gone, time slipping away
They all sing and laugh with a hip hip hooray
But despite your ill-will and feelings of grey
You have to admit, it's a Happy Birthday

Sigh (A Melancholic Farewell)

sigh

I spy
With my little eye
A reason to pry
She says it isn't so but she's not very sly
Evidence piling up making me want to cry
I knew that was an overly friendly guy!

sigh

Oh my
From the highest highs
Now I'll never fly
Beaten and bruised, in this cage I will lie
Wishing and praying to look at the sky
Knowing deep down that this is where I die

sigh

Goodbye
I will not comply
You aren't my ally
All my hopes and dreams may have gone awry

But no longer from the monster will I shy
You have no power as long as I try!

Goodbye

Biding the Tide

Moon queen in the sky, hanging so shyly above
Moon queen up so high, sing for all you love
Moon queen judging thee, penance paid is great
Moon queen choosing me, I fight against my
fate
Moon queen softly speaks "There is no need to
fear"
Moon queen makes me weak when she calls me
dear
Moon queen has to go, she says she'll always
cherish
Our love will ebb and flow, but it will never
perish

Id Entity Crisis

Siren's song steadily sinks south
Abstract anger abruptly acquiesced
Liberty lacks, liability looms
Language, laws, life, lost
Youthful yang yelling yield... Yes

Conquering Madness

Always reaching for life's own cherry
Yet the path ahead may seem scary
Faced with many great adversaries
Striving to feel that sweet false berry

All your life you have been small and weak
Abhorred and hated, scorned as a freak
It's clear acceptance is what you seek
Maybe you'll find it up on the peak

Cold and alone, feeling abjection
You can't escape your own reflection
Every feature an imperfection
But she only responds with affection

Climb to the skies with your newfound twin
Against all odds, you knew you would win
The journey ends so life can begin
Two become one, a new Madeline

Ingram Content Group UK Ltd.
Milton Keynes UK
UKHW020818060623
422954UK00016B/947